MINECRAFTERS ESSENTIALS HANDBOOK

Collector's Edition

Table of Contents

Essentials Handbook: The Collector's Edition

You now possess the most insightful, powerful, and inspirational guide to all the essential and valuable information of Minecraft ever created! This guide will feature some of the most ambitious and powerful methods and ideas that will help keep you alive!

This special Collector's Edition features exciting new content that is sure to blow you away! The carefully selected articles presented will change the way you think about Minecraft forever!

Introduction

There are many dangers in the world of Minecraft, but knowing about them ahead of time can keep you safe! Here are a few tips to keep you safe while exploring or building!

Collector's Bonus Section: Essential Guide to the Nether!

In this special Collector's Edition section, we will discuss all the essential tips and tricks to being successful in The Nether, which is Minecraft's lava-filled version of Hell! The Nether is accessed from a Nether Portal, which is a 4 x 5 obsidian rectangle activated by flint and steel!

Ladders Help You Up!

The Nether is known for its steep, daunting walls, which would usually take forever to climb! Using ladders, however, is a much underrated method to scaling these walls quickly and safely!

Save the Glowstone!

If you have ever gone glowstone mining, you will know firsthand how hard it is to collect the glowstone before it burns in lava! However making a small platform below a glowstone vein will catch all of your harvested blocks, keeping you and your loot safe!

Ghast Blast

Ghasts may be the most annoying mobs in Minecraft! They constantly shoot fireballs at you, causing you damage and disrupting your task! Counteract these attacks by building a small cobblestone wall around where you are working!

Drink Your Milk!

Wither hunting can be a very dangerous activity, but it has a very high payoff (a beacon!), so it may be in your best interest to bring a bucket of milk along on your adventure! Drinking milk will stop the Wither poison from damaging you, making it easier to fight!

Light Is Your Friend

Monsters cannot spawn in the daytime, and spiders won't chase you unless you hurt them first. So make sure to do your building when the sun's up!

Skip the Night

You can make a bed out of three pieces of WOOD PLANK and three pieces of WOOL on a crafting table. You can right click to sleep in the bed when the sun goes down, skipping directly to morning.

Light the Way With Less

Torches cast enough light to keep monsters from spawning for 7 blocks. To be safe, place a torch every 5 blocks and alternate walls!

In Case of Medical Emergency

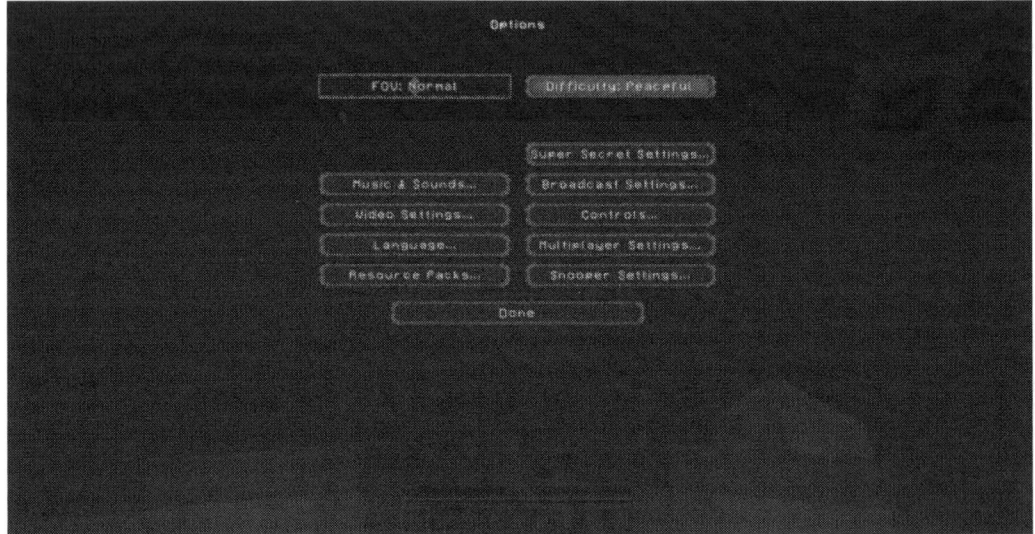

If you find yourself really low on health, open the options and set the game to peaceful. This will cause all the monsters to disappear, giving you time to eat and regain your health.

Always Bring Food

Unless you're playing in creative or peaceful mode, always be sure to bring food. If you get hungry your health will start to drop!

Meat! It's What's For Dinner!

While any food will fill up your hunger meter, meat will fill it the most and cause it to empty the slowest. Be sure to cook it in a furnace for best results.

Farming for Food

Always be sure to have a farm at your base that grows wheat. You can use three pieces to make bread, and you can replant the seeds for more wheat. Infinite food!

Hydrate Your Farm

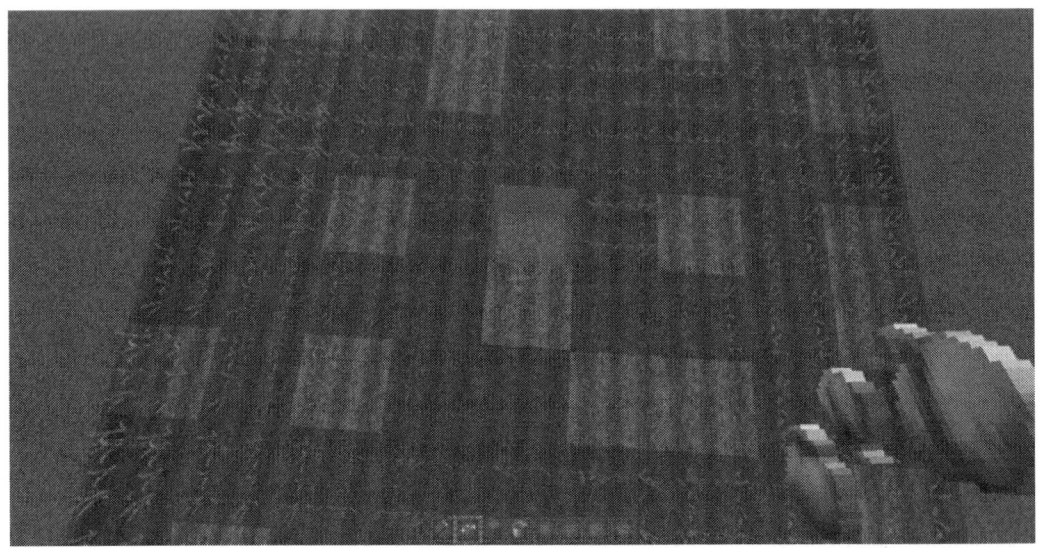

Water will hydrate farmland (make it look darker) up to four blocks away. Crops planted on hydrated farmland grow faster!

Light Your Farm

Be sure to put plenty of light in your farm,
that way your crops can grow through the night!

Protect Your Farm

Build a fence around your farm to protect it from invading monsters. While they won't take your crops, if they jump they can destroy your farmland.

Build a Greenhouse

You can build a simple greenhouse to really protect your crops by using glass for the ceiling! This will ensure that NOTHING can get in! Be sure to include a door or gate so that you can get in!

Stack Chests

You can stack chests directly on top of each other to save space. Just right click on the wall to place the chest instead of the ground.

Label Chests

Use signs or item frames to label chests so that you know what's inside!

Cheap Redstone Lights

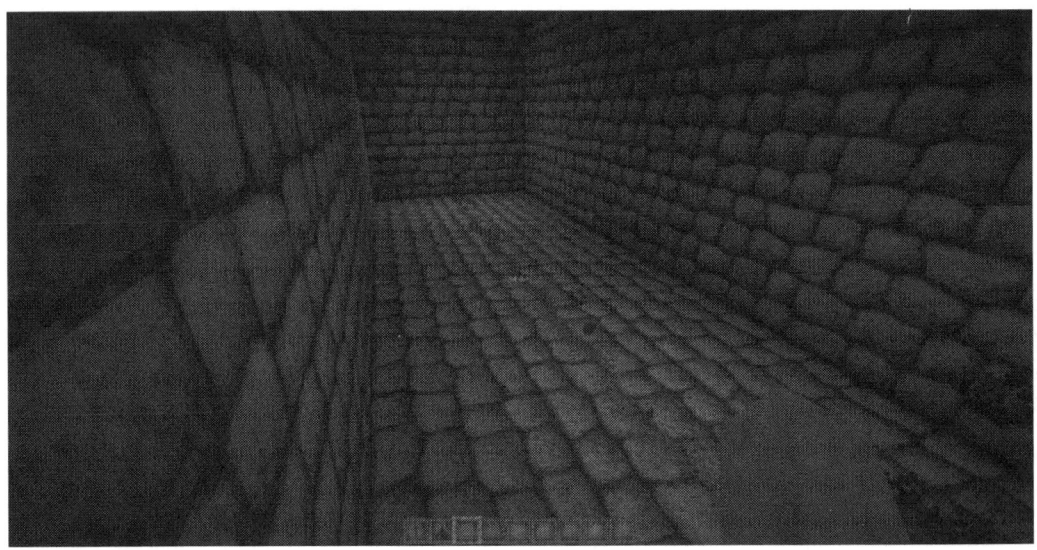

Have tons of redstone and need to light a tunnel? Lay out the redstone in a line and activate it with a redstone torch to easily light the whole path!

Stop Spawning!

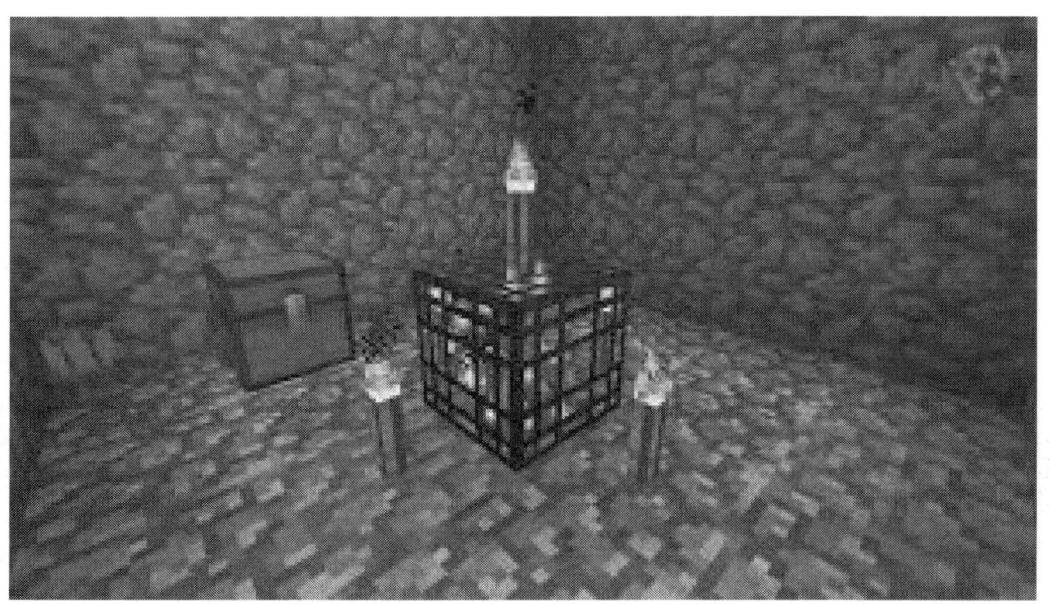

You can keep monster spawners from creating monsters (without destroying them) by surrounding them with torches. Just don't forget the one on top!

Bring Your Armor

Never leave home without a full set of armor if you can. Even leather will help to protect you!

Stay In Tip-Top Shape

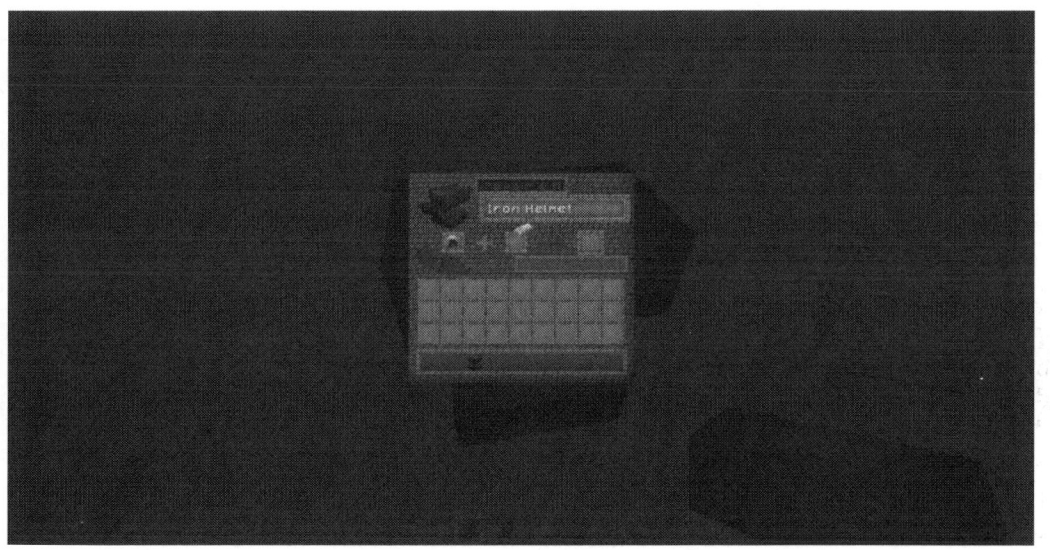

Make sure your armor is repaired before going on a long trek. Use an anvil and one piece of leather, iron, gold, or diamond (whatever your armor is made or) to repair it!

Get Your Shimmer On!

Not only will enchanting your armor give it a pretty shimmer, but it will also add valuable protection, like reducing fall damage or allowing you to breath underwater longer!

Protect Your Horse

If you've already got yourself a horse, why not protect him with armor? You can only get horse armor from chests in dungeons, but it's well worth the search!

Build a Moat

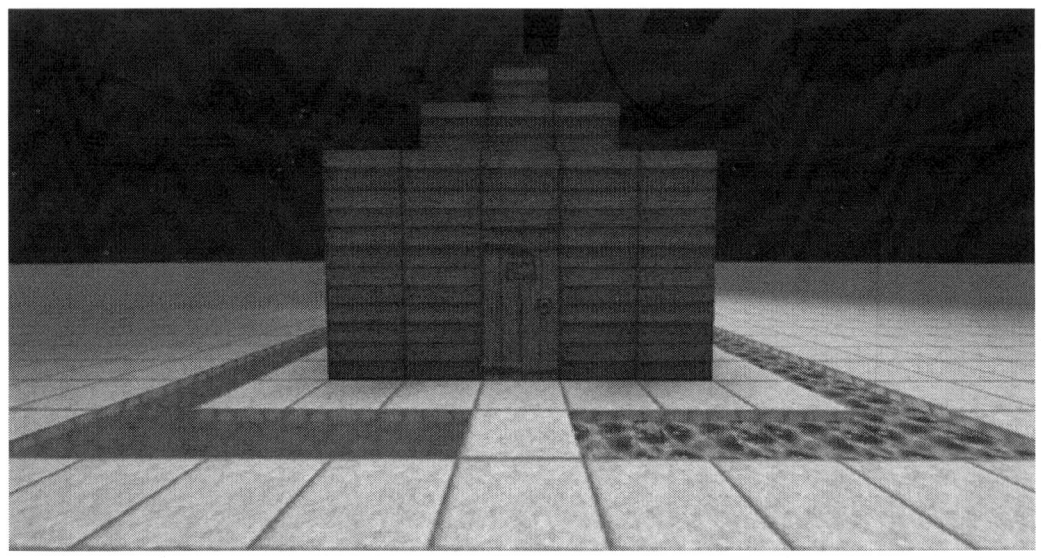

Not only are moats cool, but they'll slow down the monsters trying to get into your base, giving you time to shoot them or run away. For extra protection, try filling the moat with lava instead of water!

Surrounded by Water

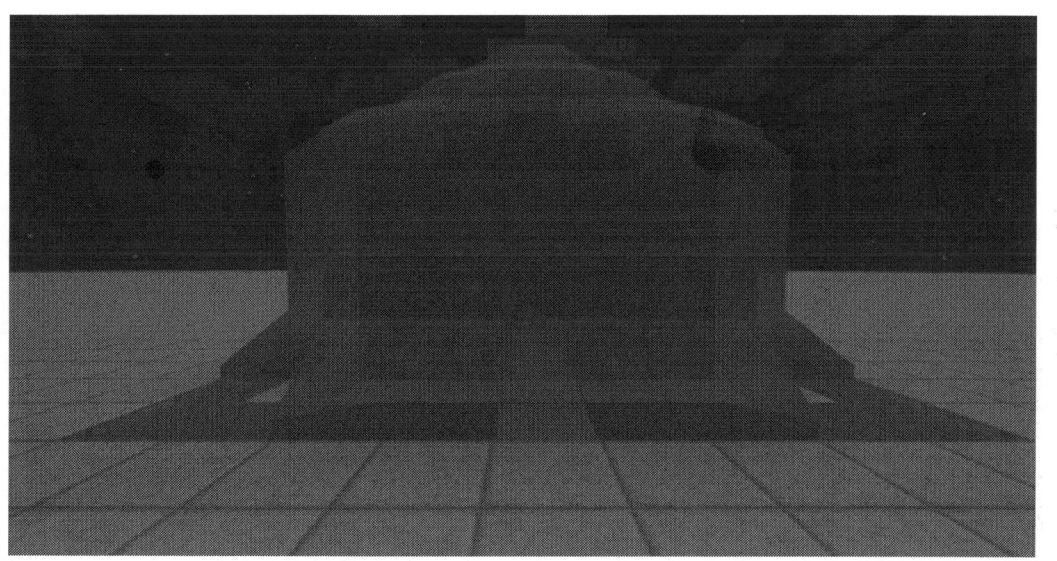

By surrounding your house with a layer of water, you can protect it from exploding Creepers! Water absorbs the explosion so that your building can stay in one piece.

Always Carry Water

You've already got your food, torches, and tools for your exploration, but don't forget a bucket of water. This handy tool can work as cheap and easy ladder or help save your life if you get set on fire!

Infinite Arrows

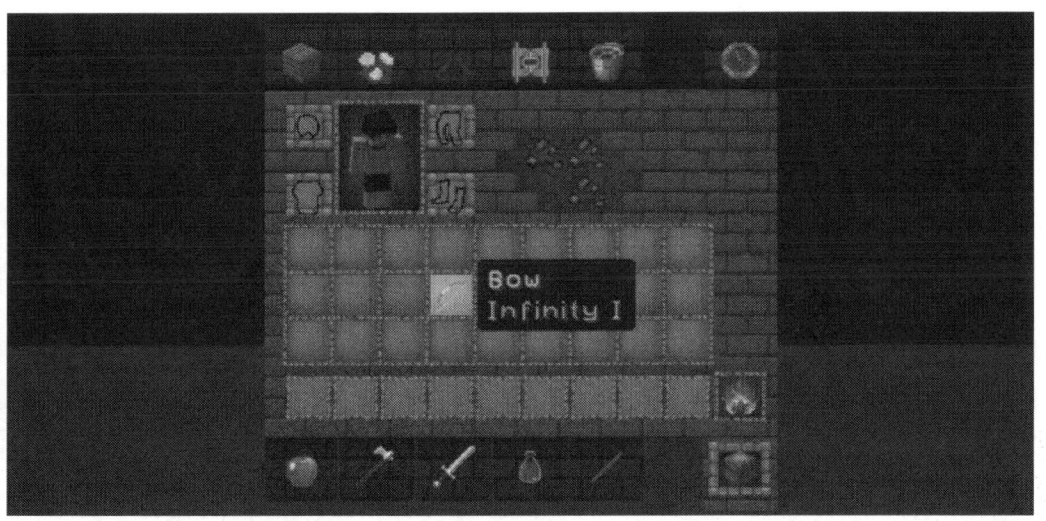

The Infinity enchantment is by far the best enchantment bow that you can put on a bow. It allows you to shoot infinite arrows as long as you have one in your inventory! This is a must-have for fighting the Ender Dragon!

Build a Hidden Door – Part 1

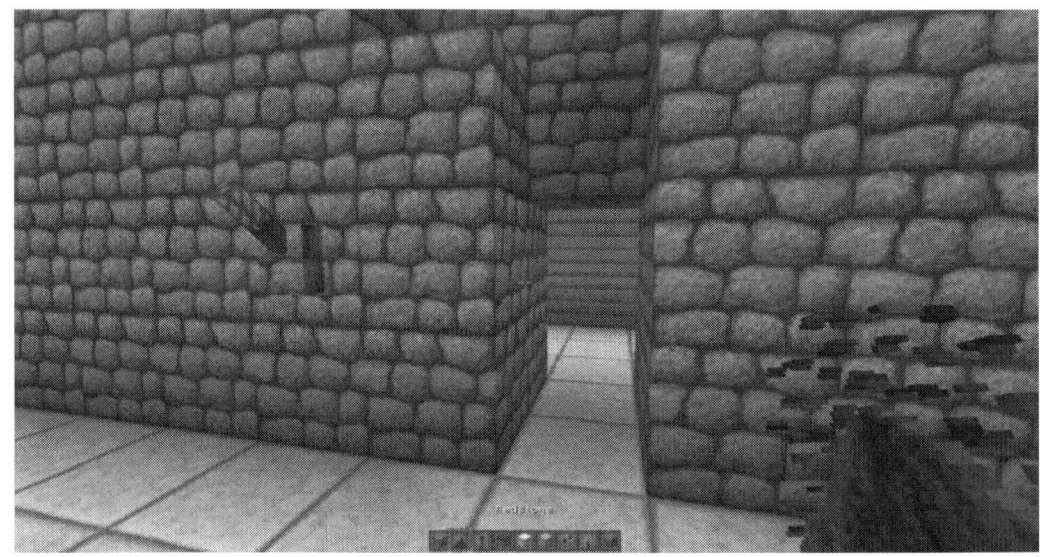

A secret entrance to your base can go a long way towards keeping unwanted visitors out. Even if you're playing alone, a hidden entrance can just be plain fun! The next few pages will explain how to build a very simple version.

Build a Hidden Door – Part 2

You will need: 2 sticky pistons, a lever, and 3 of blocks of your choice. For best results, use something that occurs naturally where you're building the door!

Build a Hidden Door – Part 3

Place the items as pictured and activate the lever. The two blocks in front of the sticky piston will move to "close" the door. Turning the lever off will "open" the door!

TIP: The piston will extend towards you when placing it, so make sure you look the right way!

Build a Hidden Door – Part 4

To finish, just place blocks to hide the door (pictured as blue wool above) and you're done. Now you have a hidden door that only you know about!

Temporary Housing – Part 1

Sleep in the sky! This is a great design for a temporary house because it cannot be touched by mobs! All you need is some ladders, stone and a bed! Don't forget your torches!

Temporary Housing – Part 2

You can only sleep at night

This house is perfect if you are low on resources, all you need to do is dig! This house should be very well lit, and you need to make sure there's no mobs inside!

Temporary Housing – Part 3

This house requires the most material, but it looks great and is very functional! An island house keeps mobs out, but lets you get to land quickly!

It's a Long Way Up!

Always bring ladders into the nether with you, they help a lot when you are trying to mine quartz or glowstone!

Pets on Leash, Please!

Prevent your horse from running away by using a lead! Tie it up to a fence to keep the horse safe.

God Save the Pickaxe!

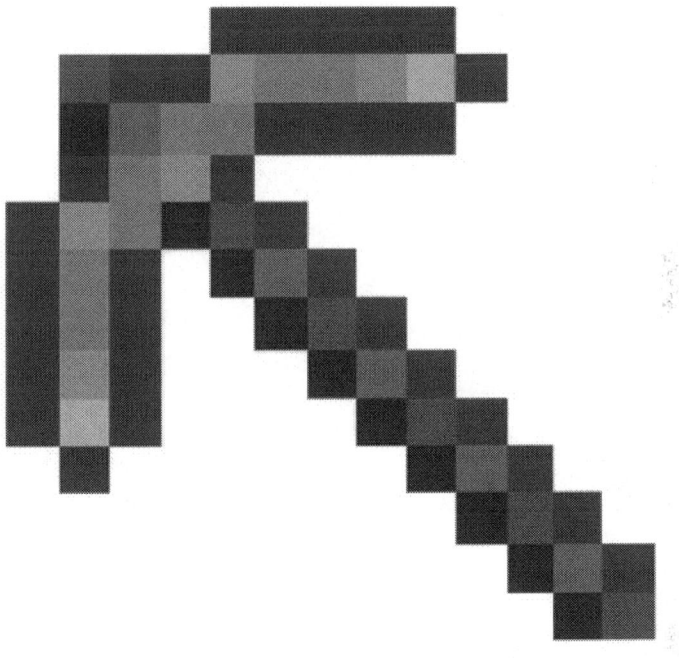

If you are low on diamonds, skip crafting a spade or sword and got straight to a pickaxe! The diamond pickaxe is much more valuable to have, as it is very heavily used and it is almost 3 times as durable as iron.

Know your Enemy!

It is important to know which weapon works best against each mob. Bows are the best against creepers and skeletons, while zombies and spiders should be killed by a sword.

Lock Up Your Valuables, Please

Put your most valuable items in an enderchest! Enderchests cannot be broken by explosions, and items can be accessed from any chest!

Automatic Farming – Part 1

Tired of harvesting all your wheat? Follow these steps to build a simple automated farm!

Automatic Farming – Part 2

   Here's what you'll need: 4 sticky pistons, 4 Redstone Repeaters, 7 pieces of Redstone, 1 Lever, 1 Hoe, and 14 blocks of your choice.

Automatic Farming – Part 3

Start by laying out the Sticky Pistons in a row as shown in the picture.

Automatic Farming – Part 4

Place the Redstone Repeaters as shown so that they are facing the Sticky Piston's backs. You don't need to increase the timer at all.

Automatic Farming – Part 5

Add the Redstone in a line to the Lever. You don't need to put the Lever on a block, but it helps to hide the Redstone.

Automatic Farming – Part 6

Place blocks in front of the sticky piston and turn on the Lever.

Automatic Farming – Part 7

Place blocks above the extended Pistons in the pattern pictured.

Automatic Farming – Part 8

Fill the space between the blocks with water. For best results, make sure each space is filled with a source block.

Automatic Farming – Part 9

Next add your farm. Skip one space next to the Sticky Piston blocks, then build the farm 6 blocks out and 4 wide as shown. Be sure to put a wall of some kind down each side!

Automatic Farming – Part 10

Last, plant your seeds and wait for them to grow. This farm will work with Wheat, Carrots, or Potatoes!

Automatic Farming – Part 11

Once everything is grown, turn off the Lever and watch the harvesting. Pick up your seed and wheat, turn the Lever back on, and replant to do it all again!

Can't Believe It's Not Butter!

It is useless to craft gold into armour of tools, as it breaks very quickly! Save gold for things such as golden apples and powered rails.

Blaze Be Gone

Fire Resistance potions work against blaze attacks! Chug one down before killing some blazes to stay safe!

Cow's Gift

Drinking milk will cure poison! If you have been bitten by a cave spider or attacked by a witch, make sure you have a bucket of milk with you.

The End

There is a way to complete Minecraft in survival mode, and that is to travel to The End and Defeat the Ender Dragon!

Finding The End

In Survival Mode, it is only possible to reach The End by finding a Stronghold. Strongholds contain an Ender Portal, which will transport you to The End! To find a strong hold, just use the Eye of Ender! Throw one in the air and it will show you the way.

Where Am I?

Use maps to make sure you don't get lost! To make a map, you will need a compass and 8 pages of paper. To use the map, just right click!

Straight out of Harry Potter!

You can use enchantment tables to cast spells on your tools! You see that green bar at the bottom of your screen with a number above? Those are your XP points, which can be used to enchant!

Barter King

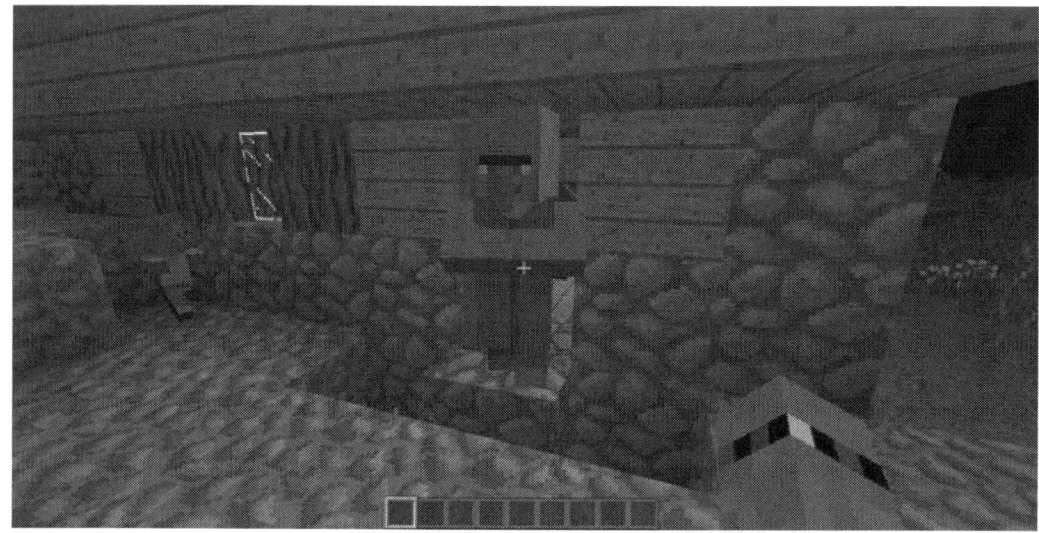

Villagers provide unique trading opportunities! You can get very rare items by trading with villagers, including emeralds!

Don't Waste Diamonds!

Instead of breaking diamond ore with a regular pick, use a pick enchanted with Fortune 3! This enchantment allows you to gain up to 4 diamonds per ore! This enchantment also works on all other ores except iron and gold.

Fuel Sources

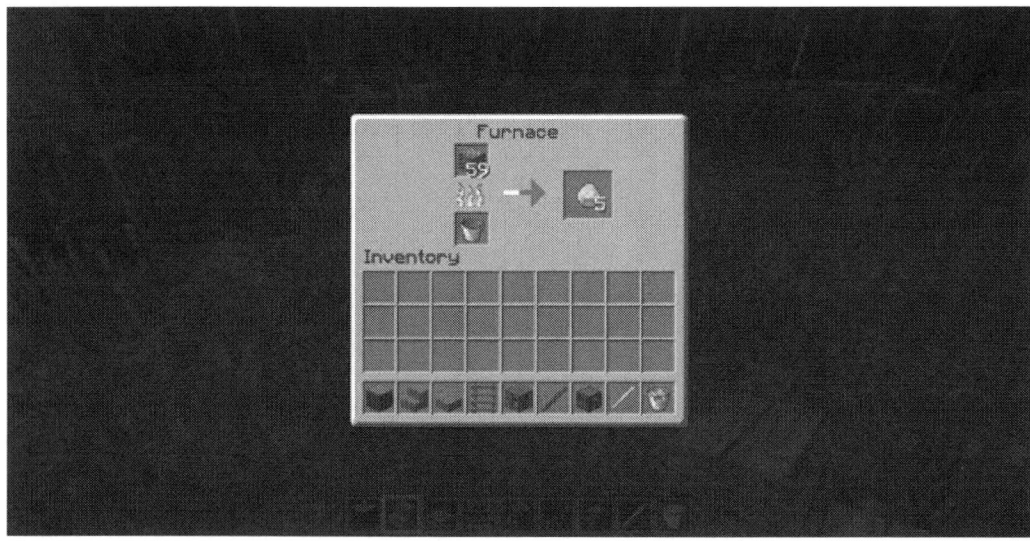

Almost any item made out of wood can be used in furnaces, except boats, signs and tools! Lava Buckets and Blaze Rods can also be used to smelt down your goods!

Save Your Energy!

It is a common habit to jump when you are running! However, it may seem like you are moving faster, but you really are not! Jumping also consumes much more energy.

Rock Bottom

There is a layer of a special block at the bottom of any Minecraft world. It is called bedrock. Bedrock is unbreakable in survival mode, so don't spend hours wasting your tools on it!

Mining – Part 1

There are many different methods for mining. Some are more effective, but some save your tools! This method, called Strip Mining, is when you create long tunnels, 1 block away from each other. This is best done on level 15 if you want diamonds!

Mining – Part 2

Cave Mining is another very common mining method. All you need to do is explore caves! This method usually does not get as much loot, but will save your tools!

Mining – Part 3

This method of mining is called Quarry Mining. The basic idea is to dig a large vertical hole straight down. This method usually yields the most loot, but takes the longest and damages your tools!

Mining – Part 4

This final method of mining is called Speed Mining. It is best done with an efficiency enchanted pick, and also a haste beacon. All you need to do is drop down to level 15 and start going crazy! Be careful of lava!

Conclusion

Surviving in Minecraft is no easy task (unless you are on Easy Mode!), but know you have the tools and ideas to know how to survive your first few days! Remember, be smart and don't dig straight down!

Manufactured by Amazon.ca
Bolton, ON

18607937R00042